True Happiness

"The Happiness that really got it going on."

True Happiness

"The Happiness that really got it going on."

Rochelle Coleman

True Happiness

"The Happiness that really got it going on."

Published by Fountain of Life Publisher's House

P. O. Box 922612 Norcross, GA 30010
Phone: 404-936-3989
Manuscripts submissions to: publish@pariceparker.biz

For all book orders including wholesale email: sales@pariceparker.biz

Fountain of Life Publishing House is committed to excellence in the publishing industry. The Company reflects the philosophy established by the founder, based on Psalm 68:11, *"The Lord gave the word and great was the company of those who published it."*

Book design copyright © 2014 by Parice Parker. All rights reserved.
Cover Design by Parice Parker
Interior design by Parice C Parker
Editor: FOLPH Editor's Team

Published in the United States of America

ISBN: 978-0-9904441-4-5

11.20.14

True Happiness
"The Happiness that really got it going on."

Fountain of Life Publishers House

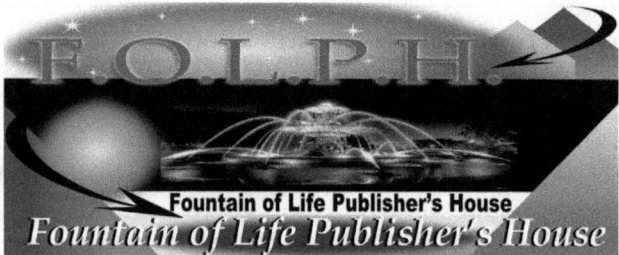

For book orders or wholesale distribution
Website: www.pariceparker.biz

True Happiness
"The Happiness that really got it going on."

DEDICATION:

I would like to dedicate this book to my children Rodney D. Riley, Aireana A. A. Carter, Dereana D. D. Carter, and my daughter from another mother Reana J. Bailey-Ballantyne. You guys gave me the reason for writing this book. I wanted you all to have a full knowledge of what True Happiness is and not base it only around certain accomplishments.

I dedicate this book to my Spiritual Mother, Juanita Bynum II, for paving the way before me and showing me different avenues to take in my life alone with living as a Christian. You are such an Inspiration in my life, and because of the Spiritual connection that we share I would always love and cherish it for the rest of my life.

I also dedicate this book to my God-Parents, Francene and Bobby Weathersby, for being my extra

True Happiness

"The Happiness that really got it going on."

supporters. They were needed in my life, especially Fran; words cannot express the deepest feelings in my heart for you, Love you ALWAYS! Most of all, I dedicate this book to my mother and father, Elder Chester and Vira Coleman, for establishing me in this world in which we live. My dad, really I would like to say thanks for "that silver spoon." Glory!

Special thanks:

I would like to say thank you to a special someone I met who gave thought to this book, Prophetess Rhonda Sharp. I thank God for your love and support throughout this process.

Table of Contents

True Happiness

"The Happiness that really got it going on."

Rochelle Coleman

True Happiness
"The Happiness that really got it going on."

INTRODUCTION

While looking over my life, I would have to say, "That on my way to pursing happiness has been a journey!" Not only that, being able to sit down while having a heart to heart talk with myself, led me to knowing that automatic happiness is more than being successful in a lot of different areas.

Today, those areas could be in being married to your dream mate, having children of your choice, all sorts of friends, having success in a career of your profession, and fulfillment in financial gain, etc.. The happiness that really had it going on in my life was when I gave God a real yes.

True Happiness

"The Happiness that really got it going on."

Now, being able to have had the chance to enjoy the different areas mentioned, there was still a yearning in me for a deeper feeling of true happiness; for a number of years, living with this thrill of happiness. Telling God yes was more than I could ever gain or achieve in this world.

So, here I am giving you some transparent information of what my journey was like and things I learned along the way.

Rochelle Coleman

True Happiness
"The Happiness that really got it going on."

Chapter One

THE
PURSUIT
TO
HAPPINESS

True Happiness

"The Happiness that really got it going on."

My walk in the pursuit to happiness started my freshman year in high school, beginning on the day of Christmas break in 1989. What a year to remember? I was living in St. Louis, Missouri at the time, and I had a moment to look upon my life while sitting in the cafeteria. I was eating my lunch and I started looking at all of the couples that were passing me by, with their gifts. Noticing, they had their mates. Suddenly, a thought came across my mind, and I said, "I too have someone to hold my hand." He also gives me gifts as well. I questioned myself, why am I looking so hard appearing as I don't receive gifts? I love seeing people happy and smiling. My boyfriend just recently graduated, and we are madly in-love with each other, so I thought. I imagined that I needed to act the part. After discovering that the one I was madly in-love with was madly in love with someone else, yes, it hurts. Sadly to say, "We jump into relationships without adding up the cost." This was my first real relationship. I drew upon his masculinity and the attention he gave me. I began to think this is not how madly in-love relationships are supposed to be. And, after having several of those kinds of relationships, I changed. I felt led to dig and to do more back ground research on the next relationship I encountered before any emotional attachments. No more rushing into serious relationships thinking or saying, "You are my boyfriend."

True Happiness

"The Happiness that really got it going on."

In my pursuit to happiness, my self-worth in a relationship was coming alive. I started reflecting on conversations about relationships that my dad and I had. See, I am a daddy's girl and he wasn't going to let nothing slip up on his baby girl. My dad and I used to take long trips away from home. We would just ride and talk, and talk, and ride. Our conversations were ... Awesome! Sitting here just reminiscing on those times of the good old days and I wouldn't trade them for the world. That was our bonding time, and I was able to ask anything that came to mind. And, Oh boy, I did! I recalled asking my dad, "So how are relationships supposed to go?" His answer forever changed my life from that day forward. He replied, "A relationship is supposed to be built with trust, love,

14

and commitments." These words gave way to a long lasting relationship with my husband, now.

I knew that in the beginning of the relationship I was made to fill like I was the only girl in the world. Nevertheless, I started doing a six month rule with them to not drop the heart all the way and learn who I was dealing with. You must figure out the way the other person thinks because looks can and are very deceiving. Noticing that only time will tell the truth. This process alone taught me a lot of preparing is needed when planning to be in a steady long - term relationship.

One Wednesday afternoon in late October during Halloween, I was out with the kids going trick-o-treating. Up walked this handsome man trying to offer them candy. Let me see, how can I possibly begin to explain what happened afterwards? Candy spreading was the opportunity of our introduction to a meaningful relationship. We begin to date and it lasted for about two years, at the most. This man was trying to be my prince charming. There were times our relationship was difficult because he was so insecure. I was just being me. He saw that he met an independent secure woman. Someone who could handle her own and stand on her own two feet without his help. He got intimidated instead of complimenting me. I was trying to win his heart and didn't need the insecurities. Oftentimes, insecurities will bring ruins to a relationship. It was hard dealing with him because he was used to women that was struck by his good looks, the way he spoiled a women, and his good sex. There go my butterflies, just by talking about him. Nevertheless, that was not enough for me. I needed much more. I wanted to make sure he was the type of man I needed. Someone who could be just like me and later on in life to see where we could become as one? So I had to say, "Well, here goes nothing to this one," too. Self-worth finally gave meaning and began to show me how I wanted to feel and to be treated in a relationship. I was finding my own voice. I knew it was needed due to all of the past-failed relationships I've had. I found it important to do that. I was looking within and being true to myself. In doing so, this gave me the satisfaction of my

17

own self-worth because I got tired of even disappointing myself. You have to know who you are before trying to make someone else happy.

One needs to look outside of self through people, places, things, money, houses, cars, fame, and fortune for fulfillment. Now that I know better having self-worth in those areas will not last. I believe that is down-right wrong! Once you obtain those things you will soon figure out that's not true happiness. Yes, getting new things make us feel good, but that's attached to our emotions. However, having peace from within and love respecting your self is an action that is exhilarating, "What I know now."

True Happiness
"The Happiness that really got it going on."

It's a great way for someone to be used and abused, by giving your powers away and your self-worth. Oftentimes, looking into relationships you have to make sure you're not lowering your standards. It will mess up your confidence anytime you lower your values so that someone can shine. Within self, you have to maintain a drive that will produce your own self-worth to shine, just like the song says *"SHINE BRIGHT LIKE A DIAMOND."* This is a true statement for anyone. In doing so, you allow yourself to maintain a sense of control over who you are. I, myself, believe this to be so true and a key factor although I have plenty I stand and live for and by. This is a motto and a belief system that I have in place for everyone that needs it in this area of your life.

True Happiness
"The Happiness that really got it going on."

Instinctively, you have to remain focused on self and always keep up with what's going on in your life. Sometimes you have to just think about self instead of your mate. You need that feeling of independence. Everyone that wants to have a more successful life needs to be independent and this has nothing to do with your mate. It is not good to always be in needy mode, this will lower your self-esteem. This invisible weapon creates its own development of you. Now, I know you do not want this to happen but a mate can be temporary. So, that is why you have to stay focused with moving forward in your life and what's going to help you maintain being self-sufficient. And, you know issues can arise that will bring about separation of some source to rain on your love life. Looking at self, and saying, "I'm nothing without them in my life." No time for a pity party and it is not an option to choose or a solution to a problem, feeling sorry for you. Self-worth is a source and a driveway for supply in surviving all mandates of one's independence that they set for themselves. There is nothing more than being so happy, and feeling remarkable after knowing that you have it going on. You feel so much better about yourself when you accomplish tasks you set out to do and achieve them. People who have set their mind up to win, have a thing with giving their credit over to others. Self worth is just what it is and sometimes to be said only by you. A bit of good old affirmation, Ha Ha…feels good don't it, LOL!

Especially, when so many are waiting on you to fail.

Now, let's look at something else too with having a sense of self-worth to your pursuit of happiness. There has to be a bit of soul seeking perspective going on that needs to take place. God, being that power source you need will give you the strength to do so.

Proverb 4: 7

"Wisdom is the principal thing; therefore get wisdom: and with all thy getting get an understanding.

Looking into the Word of the Lord with wisdom and understanding being the aspects of your self-worth.

This important tool needs to be used as your applicator to know your inner capabilities. A person knowing who they are can pull a great amount of happiness out in just about every area of their life. That is the kind of person you want to be. No matter the situation or what is going on don't let anything steal your joy. Using this form, you would always be able to obtain strength and stay strong.

This will be how you would show your strength. It is not enough to just know information concerning self-worth. It has to be accomplished in order to not have to belittle your-self. You have to keep it all together in every area. There should always be an inner strong spot within, giving navigation that will guide you. I must say, "Never lose it, reason being, it's vital to your happiness." This is really like inner self talk going on, realizing the goods that need to be stored up for great outcomes of success, for you to obtain, due to the fact that there will be levels in life to gain greater.

In these levels of pursuit to happiness, referring to relationships again, you have to watch out for affirmation. Sometime you won't get it the way you want. One way is you have to be aware of the control and amount of happiness a person gives, whether it's by giving money to control you or something else to keep you trapped. See, if you are independent you won't have worries right there. The amount of sex to control too, yes controlling with sex. It's an issue that shouldn't be. Not being careful in these area's a person can give you a sense of it, control that is, because of a person being needy, and not aware of bringing it to the table themselves. Within relationships there's another problem, insecurities, that has to be looked at as well, this is for self and mate. Levels of happiness can be altered if not addressed, that's not enjoyable. I believe this to be the number one factor that is altered, a person having this. When you learn more about your strengths and more of yourself there won't be a need to be insecure. There are levels of "feel good" in everybody. In addition, discovering is the challenge. Yes, I do believe that hard knocks can come to steal some of it, but it's retain-able. The one advantage that you have you can recover and obtain the level of authentic happiness. Yes, one can have and maintain it with dignity and joy never releasing it again. I had a special way of learning this early on while dating, in my twenties. Now, got it and gone as someone would say. There was a great purpose for me learning then because now I can teach my children and others the do's and don'ts. Sharing something else, I like to see levels of happiness evolving like a flower all coming together, just flowing. See, you have to secure your happiness with yourself first, before you can be an example or even share this discussion with someone else. Like stating before, buying things, will not cure what's going on inside of you that isn't complete. Really, nothing will help the level of happiness that one is supposed to hold. Only you have that piece to the puzzle.

More specifically, a person has to start by admitting where they are in life and not covering up what needs to take place. Humble yourself and get free. I made many mistakes in life before reaching the goals where I am today. It took me to come through this same process. As time went by in my own life, God gave me great Leaders like Bishop Scott of Lively Stone Church of God in St. Louis, MO, not even knowing himself that I would lead and Pastor one day. Wow, having a moment to reflect on the process God chose for me sent a tear down my face. No words right here blank - stare thinking…nothing but Lord, I thank you.

Okay, so it took. I got to say, "Having some morals and values, I will have to add too." Those were the perspectives that had set the tone for self-worth. Morals I would have to give credit to for directing my behavior in a lot of ways while on my pursuit to happiness. But right through here I must vividly give a shout out and give honor to where it's due to the women of God in my life in this area. During life you need them that have traveled your paths and made it out to show you the paths you can take along your journey. Given the privilege to watch them taught me how. I had seen a lot of women that had so much drama going on in their life-time and I knew that was not how I wanted to be. I had to always weigh my options to determine not to show it. Now I know that was building my character. I am glad that I went through that to show Aireana and Dereana what beautiful character looks like. If I had not modeled that in front of them, then another generation unfilled. It was not easy all the time, but I knew that a messy person and a happy person could not live in the same body. See, in my life I have seen it was essential for me to always carry myself in a certain manner and be this woman with great integrity. I had a great deal of a time making sure it happened by making sure no one corrupted it for me. I found myself always being careful of what I would say and do because it mattered. Kids of this world today need to see better examples. I will admit mine do, all of them. And others, with values, taking a look at its concept in my life. It always allowed me to look at everything in a more meaningful way. With all that has made its presence, up until now. I had searched for meanings in every matter. Incorporating this style in my personal and professional life helped me save myself from use-less time wasted. Life should always be lived on purpose and be lived with the importance of honesty, compassion, courage, modesty, forgiveness, and all the Fruits of the Spirit that's mentioned in the Bible.

Galatians 5:22

But the fruit of the Spirit is love, joy, peace, long-suffering, gentleness, goodness, faith, and so on in

(Verse 23) meekness, temperance, against such there is no law.

Life lived in a different realm I would have to say, "You reap what you sow in it," a very true saying of the wise that I have heard over and over again. Also, I would have to be the judge of that, and say, "So true." My reason being is that I have done some sowing and reaping, and, some reaping and sowing. Today I can say, "They were lessons learned and some good ones to live by." Now gathering determination, persistence, and self-discipline give way to long longevity in this carnation of field to pursuing happiness. This is a strenuous course of life, by itself. So, hopefully, this book will save you years of trouble. There is so much in it to live for. So, obtaining all this advice is needed for the journey. One of the most needed is determination being the key factor; in all matters leading to it, too. It took me striving and that allowed the best feeling ever when goals accomplished were in place. I have always said, "The key to getting somewhere and to gain, even in complicated situations, you have to start first." Unfortunately the last couple of years have been just that, complicated, but having spent many days and hours sorting out situations. I overcame using these same tactics. Going through up-hill battles with the family with their courage, compassion, and grace was part of the plan, with them being present and being able to assist, helped me to get to the other side of this.

True Happiness
"The Happiness that really got it going on."

On this journey over the course of the years, I have to pat my own self on the back for the ability to have self-discipline and be relentless. I owe it to my Heavenly Father for giving me the strength and power for it and for Him sustaining me. As I have watched throughout the years and still being able to be thrilled in every part of my being, in-spite of matters happening. I give Him all the Glory for that. It was built up in me as I went along in my life. This helped too, the Word of the Lord. I can recall a Scripture ...

2 Corinthians 3:18

"but we all with open face beholding as in a glass the glory of the Lord, one changed into the same

image from glory to glory even as by the Spirit of the Lord."

Therefore looking back that is what it was. It's how I'm making it now in my life living on by the Spirit of the Lord. Looking into being persistent is going to take away from that way too. I believe to say, as well. Going about things this way have just about out-lived every ordeal this far. I tell it everywhere I go now being persistent and I do not worry, you will get there. Sometimes, you will arrive on a wing and a prayer; perhaps, a word that resonated in your heart but through it all help comes from above. All things are possible and achievable in your pursuit to true happiness. So, hang on in there in every endeavor.

True Happiness
"The Happiness that really got it going on."

Chapter Two

ACCEPTING
YOUR
LIFE

True Happiness

"The Happiness that really got it going on."

I can recall being just a little girl, finding out what dreams and goals were. So I started imagining what true happiness is supposed to be like. Before I knew it, true happiness was leading up to a real learning experience and I was on a journey all by myself. I will call it, "The learning process." Going about it this way. I have seen a lot that I didn't want to experience even growing up. I had to start walking in that path as being what I wanted to become. My dreams were huge and I had to get more serious for them to become real. Also, what I wanted to accomplish and gain in life. I realized that time was of the essence. My pursuit was different than people thought it was set out to be. I was not looking for true happiness in all the wrong places. The hardest lesson I did learn in my life now that I am in my forty's.

My parents were very religious. My dad was the Pastor of Coleman Chapel and my mom a First Lady. She was a loving wife, wonderful mom and a very caring First Lady too. Mom gave so much of herself trying to keep the family functioning properly as well as the church. I only had one brother who is a Jr. and he was older than me. We were raised strict, but my up-bringing is one that I appreciate and respect to this day. My parents did an awesome job at raising us and I could not have asked for better parents. Although, I have to add there was more to me to be looked upon. I know that is what they were thinking. Back then, they just couldn't get a handle on it or around it, but they knew something was peculiar about me. At times, I just bust out laughing, wow! My problem growing up is I refused to let anyone tell me NO. I didn't want to hear it from nobody. I loved being in control of everything and had to have it my way or no way. It was my way or problems. I obtained that habit from my dad, but I had to learn how to submit and follow orders eventually. I remember my dad being like that, but he was much more humble than I. My mom was very classy and sophisticated. She was First Lady and that is what I experienced growing up. One who was very out- spoken and I mean out spoken! I would be thinking while she would be talking sometimes. WOW, what a mom? Do you have to tell them like that... My God, I was thinking to myself! What about their feelings? At times, I believe mom was too direct with people but at the end she got her point across.

I used to say, "I'm not going to be like that because I care about people feelings," being out-spoken I just can't do that. "Lady," is what we called her. She was just being herself and believed in telling someone what came to her mind, with no regrets. She didn't add or take away what she wanted to say. Mom just gave it to you just as it was. One thing I learned was to let people be themselves and accept them while learning how to deal with them. That was the beginning of my growing up days, accepting my life. And, mom taught me plenty and I love mom for that!

True Happiness
"The Happiness that really got it going on."

Growing up with my family and having an older brother was kind of great. Why, because me being the baby I was spoiled. Anything I wanted I received it. I got in trouble a lot by my mom because she said, "No" but afterwards I would turn to dad. His answer was always yes and that made mom furious many days. My dad called me, "Ra-Chelle" and he would say, "Go ahead Ra-Chelle." Yes, you can have what you want and my face always lit up like a cannonball. My friends would ask me back then growing up, "Why, are you so spoiled?" I was disliked by a lot of people and liked by a lot of people. I also got into a lot of fights because of that; rejected by some people for having that silver spoon. I had to let go of a lot of people in my life growing up because of the envy.

True Happiness
"The Happiness that really got it going on."

It became too much on a daily basis, to handle. I got tired of getting into fights. I began to shut myself off from many people.

My dad was a painter by trade and my mom was a nurse. I've seen a lot where they had to part-company with people, places and things just to avoid confrontation. Sometimes business matters would go in the wrong direction. They showed me too that it wasn't always wise to stay in the presence of bad company, just to prove a point. I learned to walk a way. Accepting what I believed was a better way out. Both of my parents were fighters and didn't mind telling or showing you, but then God changed their nature? Thank God, they choose better paths for situations. My parents really had a temper before they changed and I am grateful, because I started seeing the God in them both. I started seeing them do what they became. In life, I believe people become Bibles that some people won't pick up for themselves. Growing up choosing the Lord's way, my parents did it. I didn't have to experience a hard life of drugs and alcohol the way many children have. I remember well, coming home from school to my parents both saying, "So how was school today," they asked on a regular basis. I've seen stability in both of them. Those are traits my brother and I live by today. My parents being in my life made a huge difference just think all I have learned from them being a part of my everyday life. Being around through the good, bad, and the ugly too is what makes it great.

They made sure we were in a good religious environment to be able to obtain an education growing up. One thing I am sure of, your environment matters. This happens to be a great learning experience. I believe that in our day and time it really needs to be lived through many. The environment in which you live contributes too many good and bad things that go on in your life. If one has the chance to be raised in a good loving home, then one will achieve a lot. It makes their life easier and promotes them with a head start in life. The majority of families have really failed in providing that but, I know this is a need. One of the ways your environment matter, is in how positive or negative you become with a person growing up in life. Your environment can dictate where and how you end up in your life, too. It can help with plans you choose for your life and also ones you didn't ask for. The way our parents live is what guides us in the direction we must go. I noticed some people are born in negative surroundings, and then some simply choose that way of life. In fact, it is a problem also that affects your emotions. That is one of the ways a person becomes an emotional wreck, through being raised in a bad environment. Here another learning process I know to be true, your environment affects your emotions. It creeps in and takes over your entire well-being. This is not good at all. A lot of things began to be a trigger affect. Having energy that brings about a negative affect can bounce around fear in your life. In addition, it causes toxic insecurities that produce nothing but stress. Oh, not so good. Now, if this way happens to have its way, the Bible tells us:

Psalm 139:14

We are fearfully and wonderfully made.

Fear is very, very, dangerous! It causes you to not have a level head and not to think straight about things, concerning yourself. Everything around you including your sources must be positive, at all times. You want to be able to live a good and productive life.

When I got married and started to have children my mind began to wonder what we needed for a great environment. The main three is love, joy and peace. I began to think on the type of environment I wanted for my own kids. Having knowledge of everything that matters, like the community you want to live in. The kind of home you want for them, and the lifestyle, etc. I had to allow God to shine on me and in my life. He is always the center core of my life in order for me to be that special someone and guide for them all. With the help of the Lord, He's been the source for continuing all my endeavors. A mom that gleans in their eyes, forever. When you have good parents with great integrity about themselves, it helps build good character for the kids. I believe partnership from both mom and dad drives that power for a firm and good foundation for the children. This is what gives root for the children to live by once they are grown and have their own family. Although now, corporation being formed alone the entire ride from them make goals achievable even better. I can recall being on one accord and making decisions for our children especially, when something went wrong. Building a relationship with your kids will make them respect you and also follow your guidance. It has to be right in their eye-sight, too. There has to be common ground for love and respect from them about you, in order for that to take place. The saying is true, in-still this in them while they are growing up. Now, this is so true because if this is done, you have less disrespect out of them. One of the reasons this worked too was that I was making sure my kids were in church and once they got older they knew right from wrong. Bringing them up in this fashion paid off. I didn't have to face a lot of drama dealing with the twins or with my son. I didn't have trouble with these girls wanting to attend school every day, either. I also taught them to fear the Lord.

While writing this book, my kids are ages twenty one for Rodney and eighteen for the twins. All I am noticing is career minded kids and that makes me proud. I really have to say, "Rodney is now a great successful man does put that big smile there." Being parents that sacrificed-a-lot for them has really paid off. We had to learn and accept that We wasn't going to be able to do some of the things we wanted to in life. God made it possible for me to be able to keep a close eye on them, at all times.

True Happiness
"The Happiness that really got it going on."

Oh what and how the power of two can have over one's life. Being that my parents was always around, at the time of writing, eighty plus and still full of wisdom and knowledge. I really thank God for my dad and mom, as well. Dad was always my topping to my cake in every area in my life and mom topping the cake, laughing, and ha-ha! The power of two, if possible, is more than you can imagine. They taught me to not settle in my life. Once, a person does that, you are no longer living up to the values set out in you. This is where I'm grateful that they put that in me. It was crucial for me to have to be independent. I had to do things all by myself. This built the knowingness of how to handle being more responsible with or without assistance. If I didn't grab that aspect of life I would not have developed well. Previously, I learned people will say yes, they would help you only for you to build them. Going about thinking you need help, really you don't. Going about thinking this – this way will not help you it will harm you. You has to have enough courage to keep going with God and not people. It took faith, but continue. I knew that it was accomplished when I moved the family from St. Louis to Atlanta. I did not have any family just God. This move turned me into the vigilant women I am today, also everyone in my family. I took a stand and the chance of a lifetime that everything I needed was in Atlanta. Since moving, now we are all walking into our destiny, being able to become free in every area. Our family changed for the better. The family is

True Happiness
"The Happiness that really got it going on."

growing into what God had planned for each one of us, just living it out individually. I'm glad that I took responsibility for the family and it was just a better chance for us all. I am also glad we all stepped out on faith. I didn't want to be clinging on to a dream and a goal that was for us without seeing the outcome. This was the future that was envisioned with a restless Spirit, until we were finally here. Seeing now outcomes of nothing but pure positive action is priceless! I knew there was purpose in all of us and I was determined to pull it out of everybody. Even though there was testing to get here but taking that stand and saying the whole entire ride, nothing is impossible, having faith and believed on it, we made it.

So now I would have to say, "Wow!" Taking another deep breath, because talking about beginning again and having the guts to do it is really something. It took accepting my brand new start and actions plus my supporters gave me the extra courage I needed. Yes, referring to that, courage allowed me to unlock success. I gained a lot of positive energy in my mind-set to do what needed to be done. Thinking back, when we left St. Louis, MO, to go to Atlanta, it was snowing that Friday night and I was not through packing everything. The kids still wanted to go to school on that day and say their last "good-byes," to some close friends. The twins were so sad. They were starting another school. It meant they had to start over meeting new friends. Rodney was like, "Ma why are we leaving again?" I said, yes son, "again." He replied, "OK Ma you know best like you always do." I laughed and kept right on packing. I packed up last minute things. It started to get dark on us, but we proceeded to pack and began to pack the U-Haul Truck while it was dark. To top it off in the snow and rain that produced ice, we even had to leave some very expensive items behind. I didn't care. I just wanted to get closer to my destiny. I was adamant about hurrying up to get on highway 55 to pursue our journey.

Asking the question, "So what do you think gave way to making all of that happen?" Yes, you guessed it, accepting my life before and seeing into the future gave me all the courage to make it happen. If you guessed this, then you are correct. Once we were able to see Six Flags of Georgia, I started singing "Victory is mine, Victory today is mine." Yes, I sure did, LOL! I was singing my heart out too and it sounded so good my family even joined in with me. Being able to sing that song, felt like we had conquered the world. Having that kind of victory in my life, to say, "I moved my family to give them a better chance at life to become whatever they wanted, truly meant so much to me. I felt that opportunity was much better in ATL, than MO. Although, it was a lot I had to consider but me staying was not a compromise. At that moment in time, I had to think about leaving my mom and going very, very, far away. Yes, it was hard leaving some of my close friends like

True Happiness
"The Happiness that really got it going on."

Carmen, Yvette, and Kayan and the ones I grew up with but I had to. All my school friends, plus my home church Lively Stone, but colliding with where I was going in my mind; I still proceeded. I cried tears of joy leaving. Moving forward to gain that better sense in life took everything in me, but once I did, then that gave way to others who I knew would follow my lead and do the same. Now, since here just all kinds of favors of newness of life sprung up from everywhere for us. I love it here in Atlanta. It was a lot to accept living in a totally new town with no family or friends. However, once arrived I went straight to the Warehouse Church, where my Spiritual mother is Dr. Juanita Bynum. And, there I gained a whole new family. So, it was worth it accepting life new and old to get to

FREEDOM. True Happiness, "The happiness that really got it going on."

True Happiness
"The Happiness that really got it going on."

Chapter Three
FINDING HAPPINESS IN ALL THE WRONG PLACES

A much needed thought to ponder, you being the source of the supplier for your own happiness. So, meaning it's your job to make sure no issue in your life will put a damper on it. Making you opt out to find happiness in all the wrong places. I would like to say to this, to let nothing diminish your happiness that will allow you not to cultivate a good spirit in every moment of your life. Reason being you got to take care of your own way of feelings. It's your happiness first before you share it with someone else. This has to be dealt with before accomplishing anything. Life is always going to pass you by. It's so easy to let it slip away. Just in the nick of time. Happiness is something sought after, in everybody. We do this

True Happiness

"The Happiness that really got it going on."

in relationships, on our jobs, and other areas. I believe sometime we try too hard, and that's why we get the short end of the stick. If you really want to hear the truth, why are you searching for happiness all in the wrong places? It will come and not to be looked upon. I know, yes, one big secret, which I have stated before, now that's it!

Talking about finding it in other areas like drugs for one, no wrong. The biggest example is to look around in the world and see the damage it has done elsewhere. Please I'm begging, don't fool yourself and try it for fun, or with a mate. My answer to all of these reasons, you will still get hooked no matter the cause or the reason. See, you have to be careful around people, places, and things looking for happiness. Myself, it took me growing up and seeing what it did to outside family members; some things especially in my life. I quickly learned early on to love them from a distance, because I knew what I wanted to become. I did not want to waste my life doing something stupid. Being young the only thing of a bad habit I picked up was smoking cigarettes. I felt like it was a hard drug to me because being once I grew up and got saved for real. I didn't feel right doing it anymore. So since November of 1998, I have been smoke free. I have trusted my God throughout my time so far to save me from anything that will corrupt my TRUE HAPPINESS.

True Happiness

"The Happiness that really got it going on."

Receiving the Lord in my life when I did was so vital. Talking about crawling out of the sheets, when I did. What a wonder the Lord is? Searching for love in all the wrong places, through someone, only really wanting to just lie with you are a big mistake and as they use vain words of expressions just to get your goods is a trick. Don't allow those kinds of words because they turn into actions by you and the other party. Let's understand, SEX IS NOT LOVE! I happen to have been one of the curious ones. Yes, I started early being intimidated by words. Now, feeling real proud to say, "I didn't make that a habit and stay that a way." The word of the Lord became thick in my world and changed all my thoughts. I started speaking that I was married even before I was married. I became married to God's word. I started understanding that having sex before you were married was a sin and I didn't want to make that mistake any more. It just didn't feel right to me knowing what I knew, then after bumping my head in that area with the Lord. I gave up, because he wasn't playing. When the word of the Lord is loud and clear or else, you will listen. I, myself found out that a Love relationship with the Lord will do you just find, until? Well, well, well finding love in this some people would say, "It's OK." Nevertheless, if you really look at the weight of the matter? It's not good, when it consumes you in a matter of spending all you got and nothing is left to really show for it. Yep, you guessed it right. If, you said, "shopping." Finding Love in shopping to me can be an addiction, too. Shopping should be done in moderation and not used to calm nerves etc., a person getting caught up in shopping like that is heading in a whirl wind hard to get out of and can end up broke in their life span. Learning the aspects of your funds and knowing it takes money to make the world go around is the key but it's not going to happen if you spend it all up in shopping. I have a niece by the name of Ronicia, my only one in this world, who I raised from a little girl who was with me before Aireana, Dereana, and Rodney were born. Once she got older and realized life a little her favorite words, "You have to spend money to make money." So true, but how is one going to do that if they are not saving and spending everything they make? I spent a lot of cash investing in my own teen clothing label called ROCKY CHICS to get it up and running. It happened because I invested in myself and my niece was so right, you have to spend money to make it.

Sharing another thought, on finding love by means of playing video games, you may think it's not harmful, but it is. Playing video games when you first get out of bed in the morning is a true sign you are addictive. Also, when it is the last thing you do before going back to bed. Yes, that's an issue. The saying, "It's more to life than just playing games." Now, playing video gaming is not bad but when you become addictive to them, they become a problem. Video gaming must have its place in your life without taking it over. A life

True Happiness

"The Happiness that really got it going on."

driven by what a person has dreamed of since childhood and then growing into a man is great. But, do not let it pattern your life after playing video games all day. The ball point here is not the girls but it's the male gene because you don't really see a lot of girls playing them. The female generation has things they toil with in a nut shell all of their own, they are not really dealing with finding love in this kind of a way. Perhaps, thinking that it's real love from someone and really only what an older person would say called puppy love, yes it may be that. Thinking back on the males, my question is WHY? My answer would be to PLEASE have some since of balance with these gaming gadgets, warning… (SCREAMING OUT LOUD) OK I'm back! I guess I should not be coming down on them too bad, but I have had my share of the game playing. I needed to address that so you cannot let it get too far and turn it into finding love in all the wrong places. Although, it's wrong especially for a grown-up. I could go on and really step on some toes by saying watching too much T.V. is a problem too like sport gaming but that subject only going to say just do it moderately and in agreement with others to obtain PEACE.

Finding love all in the wrong places could make you really miss out on a lot in life, a person really needs to be in route of wanting more and able to strive after; also, fight for what it is that you are in pursuit of, or life will just pass you by all because you chose to find it on the wrong path. I myself fought against all type of odds to be where I am in life. This was the opportunity that I had to exercise patience in a lot of areas, too. I had to use it to navigate through the odds and to get to point after point that I was trying to gain. I had to endure some things and some that were really unbearable. It's such a privilege to understand and know the different tactics to use to get to where you want to be in life, but in doing so, sometimes it is going to take some sweat and tears, but at the end of a matter it's surely going to pay off, dearly. So again saying, finding love all in the wrong places, don't let it distract you and knock you off. Things will manifest itself in due time, don't get caught up in using idol time and let it take over because it can. Keep a ONE-FOCUS type of mind set and become

UNSTOPPABLE in your life. Don't quench or crumble at what you might have to face in life that would want you to turn other-wise, though it might seem like a mighty ball of fire to wreck with, just withstand and turn to your Higher Power for assistant to get through it, the process that helps frustration encountered because being human and living life it happens to us all.

So, now let's talk about identity and the "how" of the matter you are going to go from where you are to who you want to become in life. You may want to reflect on your situation at hand first and say to yourself, how did I get here in order for me to change this, then deal with it by prioritizing things in your life to gain a sense of

True Happiness
"The Happiness that really got it going on."

where you are headed. Getting a clear judgmental mind-set on steps is very important. Talking about my own identity, I can think back one time in my own life when I was hanging around a crowd that was really not my cup of tea. It was due to the life style they lived and I had to use these same rules and apply them to my life to change my own matters for the better of me. This was a hard decision due to one of them being my cousin but I had to think back on the life I was trying to have and think on if I stayed in that crowd of people that I could end up in life some where I didn't want to be. I had to get a grip on myself. I can say that back then is really where, in my life, I respected and loved that I had a God-mother. Fran didn't play about me and found out that I was living a certain type of way and hanging out with them and stepped in my life like a wrecking machine and demanded that I quit hanging around those people; she sat me down and talked to me and gave in-sight on a lot of things for me that helped me see things clearly. After doing some of what she said and wanting to change, things got better and I was back to myself. I don't think that back then it had to become a magical experience, I just had to sit and think about me and who I really was. As energy flows become zealous enough to always think of you and not be overtaken by surprise of others that may take you off into a realm you really don't want to be. I say this not just because of the sake of it but the zeal of who you are always. Let it be on the forefront of your life to not become bored with living a good one. Don't ever lose the strength of it. Now, I look forward to always doing a self-check to make sure I'm moving in the right direction I want to be in my life. It really makes you feel some type of way in a good sense.

Speaking on making use of preparation in life to make sure you don't end up finding love all in the wrong places me-myself, spend a lot of time alone, this I used to gain that power that was buried on the inside of me to come up to the surface who I was with no distraction. I also used to get into my truck and have music a-float and just drive, sometimes down the highway out of town. This was very therapeutic for me, time to let my mind wonder on any thought that came to mind. This was something that I saw was a good habit that I picked up and this is something I still do in my life right now to this day. I needed the time to be able to go back and forth with things that were on my mind and this way makes me bring about that answer needed or just clarity. Getting in my truck and going to the mall or some other type of store wasn't doing it for me, I had to go on long trips, and after doing so, very beneficial. My mom used to ask the question why do you have to run up and down the highway, and I would say back to her it's one of the ways that I relax my mind to get a clear one. I can add now, going through life you need something in a good form of a way when you are trying to go to the next level in it. Going about in my life in my late twenties and some of my thirties it seemed like I was always in a boxing ring and needed to have a time-out to re-group. I did it so much back then it became a part of our life to take road trips. My kids, plus my niece started enjoying the rides and would sometimes ask, OK so, when is the next one. I began a trend and started my closest friends to start going as well. I can say, too that now in my life it's not so much of a demand but I still enjoy the ride for some fresh air. Schooling life as the world would say, it calls for some type of stability and the time-frame for building a developmental system, so slowing down from the drive so much became my way of life in my late thirties.

True Happiness
"The Happiness that really got it going on."

I heard it over and over again before I started using the same regiments, the Bible states in Habakkuk 2:2 "and the Lord answered me, and said, write the vision, and make it plain upon tables, that he may run that readeth it." That's the plan, to write down your vision and make it plain, meaning to go and decree and declare a thing. The saying is really true. You can have whatsoever you say. You might have to put in the work for it. The possibility of having it is achievable. All you have to do is put in the time alone with the work and effect, you will be successful. The Bible states again "the just shall live by faith" and this tool too, is needed yes, faith. I do believe in see it and say it visions, also as well as the plan, and it shall be done according to that. I'm helping my children with this one while watching them grow into adults. I'm repeating to them all the time now, to trust in God because you will need him in life. I'm telling them every day you bear fruit doing it this way from Him. I had to show them through my life that a life spent in love with Him - He proves Himself well. I take no pleasure in it for the credit of what He has done in my life. I give all the Glory to God.

The reason for this book, TRUE HAPPINESS is the set of words I am so passionate about writing, but I wanted to make sure I was being effective in my communication of conveying not only through words but actions, too. Actions will always speak louder than words. I had to allow my kids to see this with what I did in my own life because they became these kids that did everything they saw me do. I didn't want to be the type of parent to tell my kids you do as I say, not what I do. I wanted them to see it by example in me. I became a living Bible right before their eyes. I said to them all, you guys will know how to conduct yourselves once you get grown and on your own, so finding love all in the wrong places really isn't something you want to add to your life to make you live a different way in it. The trend has to repeat itself with their own kids to show them how too, and so on. There was nothing so special and wonderful about me being their mom, I just only did and said as God did. I saw how it was so powerful and effective in my life by doing so, I had to pass it down to them. It was God's words that became my life and a guide to live by. Writing this book too, I believe that others needed to hear the TRUE HAPPINESS THAT REALLY GOT IT GOING ON.

True Happiness
"The Happiness that really got it going on."

Chapter Four
THERE'S FREEDOM IN HAPPINESS

True Happiness

"The Happiness that really got it going on."

*T*he journey continues, sharing "Freedom In Happiness" which is like climbing some stairs. The things in life we go through, our short coming, our daily routines pressing against forces are not close to comparing the glorious sensational thrill you get from being free. Even if it happens and you fail at something trying to get there, don't let the disappointment deter you from remaining on your way. What matter is the HOPE that you keep alive to thrive in whatever circumstances you have to go through, and once arrive, there it is, that cultivating feeling you have been waiting on...FREEDOM. I always reminded myself of this scripture in the Bible through tough times like this and in **1Corinthians**

True Happiness
"The Happiness that really got it going on."

4:17 "For our light affliction, which is but for a moment, worketh for us a far more exceeding and eternal weight of GLORY." This was what I found to be so true anything is nothing but a light thing if you can see it that way. This saying in the Bible lets you know to not let anything bind you up in no shape, form, or fashion. Telling the truth concerning this, I had to tell myself this a lot because of obstacles always being in my way, this journey wasn't easy sometimes. I must say you will have to fight but know that FREEDOM feels better than any other temporary feeling. Yes I know that sometimes you can be wrapped up so tight in a person, place, or thing until really you have to think for a moment, there is something for me called FREEDOM as long as I have breath in my body, then is where you say, let the fight began. Having "FREEDOM IN HAPPINESS" doesn't have to be, but again, sometimes you do have to fight to get the freedom you require.

Generally speaking, remembering being free, but recalling one particular act in my life that caused a whirl wind effect and things started happening back to back and the advantage I had was I knew what it felt like obtaining it. I thought about it over and over again how I got to FREEDOM and went to that place in my life of familiarity to get it back. There was no quiet approach that had to happen. I had to become highly assertive and get back what once was mine to begin with. I couldn't blame others for what happened to me instead I used positive energy I knew would work for me. The approach I took gave me the assurance to know I was going to be ok in the end. It took some adapting but those periods were long, I just had to maintain through it all and remain prayerful.

So, we all know that going through, that there could be a possibility that we as a people could change, well at least your character is challenged. Your personality can take a turn for the worse. Though timing I believe is not so bad, you just have to encourage yourself until you are back to the feeling of FREEDOM, and don't panic under pressure, you'll make it, and after that, a note to self, always remember it's your job to make

True Happiness

"The Happiness that really got it going on."

yourself happy and NO ONE ELSE, place or thing, first. I call it the freedom release-R to any and everything that you can imagine to happen to put a damper on who you were born to be.

Having learned a little about FREEDOM, see it caused for that assurance to be on the fore-front of everything. If it wasn't for it, giving up would have been real easy. There, lying ahead, are too many opportunities in front of me to do such a thing, so I didn't. Having my thoughts guided in the right direction is what kept me going. I believe that's where my power source was in, my thoughts, as I say to whom is reading, is to be careful and live with integrity, no matter what's happening. While learning too, I knew that having that poster of preparation was always going to have to stand out. I can say that meant to me I had to protect myself and watch my inner circle. The people around you are important because whether positive or negative words are spoken, they are going to affect someone, but you have to be keen to your senses to know the difference.

Freedom in happiness brings about this liberating feeling that's unexplainable at times. To me, it's even more than a feeling of liberty. With liberty being about the ability to do whatsoever you want, meaning you do have rights. Freedom in my eyes is very important because I'm able to live my life the way I want to and not have it chained down in any type of way. I also believe, I don't have to live in such a way that's not wanted by me. I really love this life in which I live. The freedom in happiness that's going on in my life has been earned. It's a choice I made. One of my own, the ability to make the reasonable answers in everything I do to be happy and do it without fear. Now, I understand in the Bible where it states in 2 Corinthians 3:17 'Where the Spirit of The Lord is, there is Liberty, yes that's true and helpful a whole lot. This stops the sense of longing for happiness to begin with. So now, you have to turn to yourself and ask, self what does freedom in happiness mean to me now that she has explained hers. I can answer one of those ways, just truly blessed and having so much joy and peace in life that it has to offer in this present world. Yes! That's it!

True Happiness
"The Happiness that really got it going on."

One of the major influences in my life is Ambassador Doctor Juanita Bynum, who was one that spent a life-time becoming one of the wisest women of our time. She has taken me as one of her Spiritual daughters, which I have considered a very great honor. Her advice on happiness has often been sought after by both men and women of all nationalities. Her knowledge on freedom is powerful, as well. She has helped people of this world to lead them into becoming what so ever they wanted and have success with it. For a number of years now I have looked up to her. She is also one of the reasons I'm able to have the wisdom and the strength and power to put it all together by thought to write this book of my forty years, so far. I have said and believe this to be true, too, that as

True Happiness

"The Happiness that really got it going on."

long as I'm on this earth and serve God and keep him first in my life, freedom and happiness will always be mine. The saying I like to "As a man thinks in his heart, so does he become." I have learned to that whatever I do is a reflection of my thoughts, so now, all of my life experiences are patterned after nothing but happy thoughts to gain results of any solution needed.

There's freedom in happiness sometimes, for some people it may take a minute. Don't ever throw in the towel on it, because little by little it will happen. The more you change your mind, the more you began to walk in that way. I know there could be so many opportunities that are tremendously large to do so, but if you hold on and grip with fortification, you would have what you're after. In my own life I had to pull from this same perspective not once but many of times. Taking a moment to laugh at myself, I was one of those who learned a lot by their own mistakes. It may sound crazy to learn from falling flat on your face but yes that's how I got a lot of lessons, sometime. I would have to say here, that I let myself heal and then returned again, yes I did. The learning came after I said I don't like the healing process, it's too long, plus time on my hand to stop and think made me whip my own self, and that allowed me to not want to repeat the process all over again. Thinking about issued faced, I can recall when I was in the hospital because I had gotten shot in my arm. The path of freedom in happiness I thought I had because I was able to do what I wanted to do and hang around people who I wanted to as well, oh, but what, I was wrong. Once I healed from that I had to change the flow of the way I did things in my life and that meant change people, places and things. Now this is the empowerment of it all, changing your walk of life for a path of happiness. You live a life of going about it the way you see fit but sometimes the way you take may not be the right way. Whatever the answer may take some logically thinking on your behalf. Myself having to do this as well, I know for you it will take the same and that's God you are going to have to gain from. Too many influences can cloud you having what you want. The guide coming from him leading you in the right path will give you the desires of your heart but it's truly your decision to make.

True Happiness
"The Happiness that really got it going on."

Chapter Five

HAPPINESS
ABOVE
CIRCUMSTANCES

*L*ife above circumstances should be lived full of joy, but that's not always the case. There must be a rest in True Happiness that God wants us to have in order to do so. Given truth about it, circumstances can put a stain on it. Think about it as a diamond being made. The mistake not to make is to let your happiness be pending upon your circumstances, really the bad ones. Know that life is still expecting something out of you, what is for one is totally different from others in a given life. You have to learn to distinguish what's best for you and sometime in a most creative way that gives meaning to you. Now, emotionally speaking, even when there's a temporary refinement placed on oneself is realized, the duty still becomes yours to not act like all hope is gone. You have to remain conscious enough at all times to mustard up strength to fight against all odds and find beauty in spite of it. This is vital to recovery out of that refinement. I know first off, reason being, I had some health crisis I had to face…Oh yes I did. The circumstance that's even thrown at you, sometimes just the cares of life alone will take your breath away. Yes, it will; do not allow it to choke the life of happiness out of you. As we flow through life, it's going to be there. However, learning the smart way to navigate your way is the key answer here. From my perspective, getting older and watching your body change as you age is something that can take the breath out of you and throw it out the window, but again, don't

True Happiness

"The Happiness that really got it going on."

let it. As I have gotten older I became wiser. Being able to write this book in my late thirties was phenomenal for me. Watching the process unfold made life a little more meaningful to me, really when I can look over my twenties and thirties and see that life was just real are the reasons that made this book so well written. It feels so good to say I made it out of the first half of my life with "True Happiness, the happiness that really got it going on."

Now, the circumstances that come along with taking care of love ones, a touchy subject and a joyous one at the same time, too. The timing of this writing happens to be when my dad, the Rev. who is eighty years young, I will have to say.

True Happiness

"The Happiness that really got it going on."

Another stepping stone in my life, my dad told me in one of our daughter daddy moments to not throw him away in some nursing home if I can help it and the timing too of writing this page, dad had a stroke and watching him go through it was tough for my eyes to handle but seeing God pull him through it just amazed me and not having to put him in a nursing home for good, I was so happy. Dad, Chester looked me straight into my eyes and said those words again… don't throw me away. I myself remembering in my mind the years I have been here on this earth and daddy never taking a break or leaving me without his help when needed, so I knew that the Lord was saying it's your responsibility now. Since taking on the role, seeing him age right before me, I cry, laugh, and smile all at once, sometimes, especially after his stroke, thinking that one day God is going to need him and call him home. I enjoyed all of my days. Recalling moments with him, my dad being there when I got shot in my arm with a gun, being there throughout the birth of all of my kids, being there to watch me go through a divorce with my twins' father, William, and to see me off again with my second Thomas, and to move with me everywhere God said go, my dad never has missed a beat. Now that I have accepted my call and a year later pastoring a church, Grace for the Kingdom Ministries, dad is still there, and for that I'm grateful.

The circumstances, my mom on the other hand, the happiness I feel thinking of her, alone. I can say that she was there, as well. With her not being in the same state that I live in, Atlanta, I'm not that daughter around the corner to her anymore, but will and has been a phone call away for her, if needed. The one way I know my role with her is to be that listening ear. God has really been good to her where she is able to do more for herself. As I thought about that, I thank him for it because that's a burden I don't have to carry. My mother we call her LADY, and she lives up to that name and all of the definition that comes with it, too. Yes, that's truly her, a classy lady.

All things becoming new through circumstances in life, to bring about that happiness, is really where it all begins. I myself am a real true living testimony of it, saying no matter what comes my way. The deal for me was to speak life in life. I had to learn to verbalize that after a while as I was getting older. I found out that a great source of power was released when done to live through any kind with joy, too. Seeing it new now, my life with TRUE HAPPINESS took on a different outlook on any and everything done. My new motto became "Live Life Like it's Your Last Day on Earth, meaning live it in another dimension to be able to talk about it and live each day and smile while sharing the story. This was what I began telling everyone I came in contact with, reason why, there was no need to not be comfortable to live a life that you only live once and not able to enjoy it the way you want, with also accomplishing goals and dreams.

So basically happiness above circumstances of life, will take determination, because you are automatically recording everything that's going on in it. Just saying something in your life can be good, bad and some ugly too, but being persistent gets you to see your happiness and get to the big picture of it all, I must say. Therefore, see sometimes our thinking have to be renewed. Pulling from a higher sense (GOD) is something to rely on. It states in the bible **Mark 13:31** "Heaven and earth will pass away but (Thank God for that Word) my words will not pass away." That is a legacy for happiness to know you will have it until the day you die, God's word…Wow, had to go there for a minute. I found out that it was not just a book on a shelf but a good source to live by. From the beginning to the end it will get you from earth to glory.

True Happiness
"The Happiness that really got it going on."

Chapter Six

THE
SECRET
TO
TRUE HAPPINESS

God reassured me that true happiness is having him in your life through confirmation. He always shows me examples that He is here. This blew my mind! I began to always say, "As long as God don't leave me I'll always have it." See, the process of the secret is to know that He won't ever forsake you. It is written in the Word of the Lord

(Matthew 28:20)

"and, lo, I am with you always, even unto the end of the world."

I know with all of that being said, it's not wise to say, "If I don't have this person, place, or thing going on in my life then I won't have that happiness that I desired. Taking a look over my life

True Happiness
"The Happiness that really got it going on."

back when I was around my long-time friends in St. Louis, Missouri, they would say, you go through present issues in and out of your life and you have this attitude like nothing ever happened. When I discovered that as well, it was only confirmation that I do look to God as being the one and I really don't want out of it; I said to myself, let no one ever steal that place in God from me. I owe that to myself to always remember that because knowing the real source is powerful and I have to keep that in focus concerning "True Happiness."

Psychologists argue the point that to have true happiness and for it to last forever and ever must achieve many goals, they say there's strength in it. I will always argue this point, because speaking from experience the truth speaks for itself. God! God is love and love is happiness. This is my accompanying thought concerning it. Some people talk about designing true happiness as I do, but looking into that, it can become something designed to fail and not last is the problem, with God this is not a choice by him, at all. Secondly, analyzing situations into play for your life is not the answer at all, neither. You can think until the sky turns gray; spending that time won't create it. There is only one source for the job. He's the great I Am cultivating true happiness. In fact, in the pass, God has a good track record that's been proven and given out to many, which is a real gain of happiness that over-extends to other pleasures in

True Happiness
"The Happiness that really got it going on."

your life. This brings no dissatisfaction on any level. Not even this, the impact of a lot of events going on does not compare to it as well. Yes, the human mind thinks that True Happiness is people, places, and things but, no, it's really not. Even children are being raised and also raising themselves to think so. It's time we teach them the true concept of it. Teach them that yes you can have these things but don't let these things have you. The easy way for a trick to catch you is to fall in this kind of madness and have your mindset blinded by it. Knowing God's presence will always be in your life letting that be your focal point, getting into this way of thinking and staying away from a humanistic way of thinking is really liberating. The ultimate feeling in the entire world

True Happiness

"The Happiness that really got it going on."

is when you know for sure and have confident in knowing where your happiness comes from, oh what a feeling. Not the talk of having true love or anything else, no not it, reason being God was the one who gave you your spouse, not you, remember? So, why you won't have him as your true happiness? To tell you the truth love have its ups and downs, but God's love never changes. As we know, just with everything else, there will always be problems that tamper with the way you feel about any accomplishments you have. You see, this strategy is one that can keep you in every area of your life, knowing who puts the joy in it for you and have at it with the rest of it. Trusting this way, you won't go wrong. As to this, it opens up so many more avenues to walk through happiness.

True Happiness

"The Happiness that really got it going on."

There are others that feel this way as I do, and I say keep up the good work.

I will have to add and say, that growing up in church learning about God and having a real relationship with him, I am so thankful. The Spiritual awaking of it all, loving God more is the result that came from me wanting to have that closeness with him, even though being in church all of my life, but still the relationship with him made the difference instead of a lot of head knowledge by reading although that is the beginning, reading The Word. As I began to live my life I saw that I needed him in a special way that made him real to me by his hands all in it. Walking with him side by side all these years so far; I really owe him the thanks, really for his love and kindness toward me that made me able to walk the way he had planned for me and the affection on a consistent pattern. It takes God to show you how to live your life, which paths to take and which road to go down. Being in relationship with him, He does all of that. Then I say too, I don't know about you reader, but this is a *want* of mine in my life. I will forever Praise and Love our God. All the Glory and Honor of my life I give to Him for it, past finding all of the beautiful truths someone else can tell you or even you believing it yourself. Let the concept of your entire being be stimulated and walk this whole new discovery. I know for some, WOW, such a meaning that makes sense of thought about True Happiness, the happiness that really got

True Happiness

"The Happiness that really got it going on."

it going on but be at its peak, the saying is true "as a man thinketh so is he" is the go-to here. As a being of this new way of thinking one should always have a way out of putting people, places, and things, before the main source of happiness which embarks maturity on your part. I say to you now, being able to unlock the secret to happiness in your life, let every other happiness such as in all of the ones I have written about never compare to His, GOD almighty. This will bring you nothing but joy and excitement and smiles in the very end.

True Happiness
"The Happiness that really got it going on."

Biography

Rochelle Coleman is a Pastor, business woman and author. Coleman is one of two children from the marriage of Elder Chester Coleman Sr. and Vira Coleman. She began this journey in Atlanta Georgia. She relocated from St. Louis Missouri and was born in Memphis Tennessee.

In 2012 Pastor Coleman answered the call to minister. She launched a teen clothing line called Rocky Chics and then, two years later she captured the author inside. Coleman is a very inspiring woman to many individuals.

True Happiness
"The Happiness that really got it going on."

Rochelle Coleman contact information

Email: rcreationsc@aol.com

111

True Happiness
"The Happiness that really got it going on."

www.ingramcontent.com/pod-product-compliance
Lightning Source LLC
Chambersburg PA
CBHW052128090426
42741CB00009B/1995